Your Brain

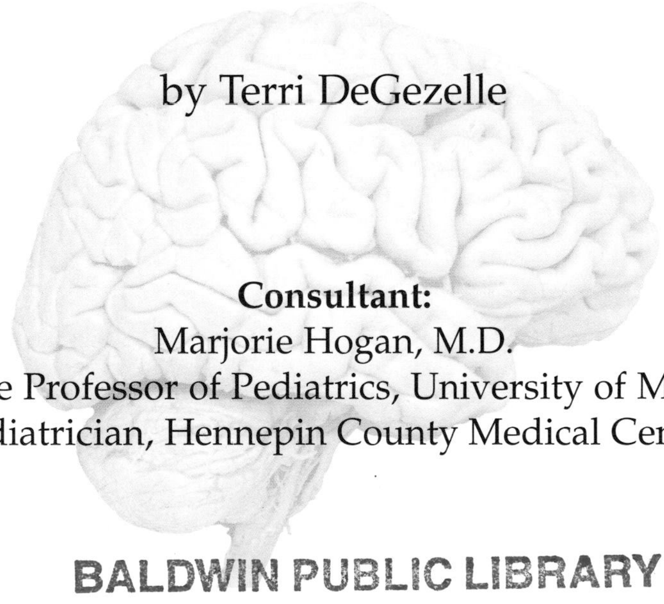

by Terri DeGezelle

Consultant:
Marjorie Hogan, M.D.
Associate Professor of Pediatrics, University of Minnesota
Pediatrician, Hennepin County Medical Center

Bridgestone Books
an imprint of Capstone Press
Mankato, Minnesota

Bridgestone Books are published by Capstone Press
151 Good Counsel Drive, P.O. Box 669, Mankato, Minnesota 56002
http://www.capstone-press.com

Library of Congress Cataloging-in-Publication Data
DeGezelle, Terri, 1955–
    Your brain/by Terri DeGezelle.
    p. cm.—(Bridgestone science library)
    Includes bibliographical references and index.
    Summary: Introduces the brain and its makeup, its function within the
nervous system, brain diseases, and how to keep the brain healthy.
    ISBN 0-7368-1147-8
    1. Brain—Juvenile literature. [1. Brain.] I. Title. II. Series.
QP376 .D43 2002
612.8'2—dc21
                                                                2001003593

Editorial Credits
Rebecca Glaser, editor; Karen Risch, product planning editor; Linda Clavel, designer;
    Alta Schaffer, photo researcher; Nancy White, photo stylist

Photo Credits
Capstone Press/Gary Sundermeyer, cover (boy), 4, 10, 12, 14, 16, 20, 22
Corbis, cover (brain images), 1
Index Stock Imagery/Frank Pedrick, 18

**Bridgestone Books thanks Wenger Physical Therapy for providing a model spine
used in a photograph.**

1 2 3 4 5 6 07 06 05 04 03 02

Table of Contents

Fun Fact

The right side of the brain controls creative talents such as music and drawing. The left side controls reading, speech, and math skills.

Your Brain

The brain is the control center for
your body. Your brain receives messages
from your body. It also sends messages
to other parts of your body. The brain
controls breathing, thinking, and
moving. It also stores memories.

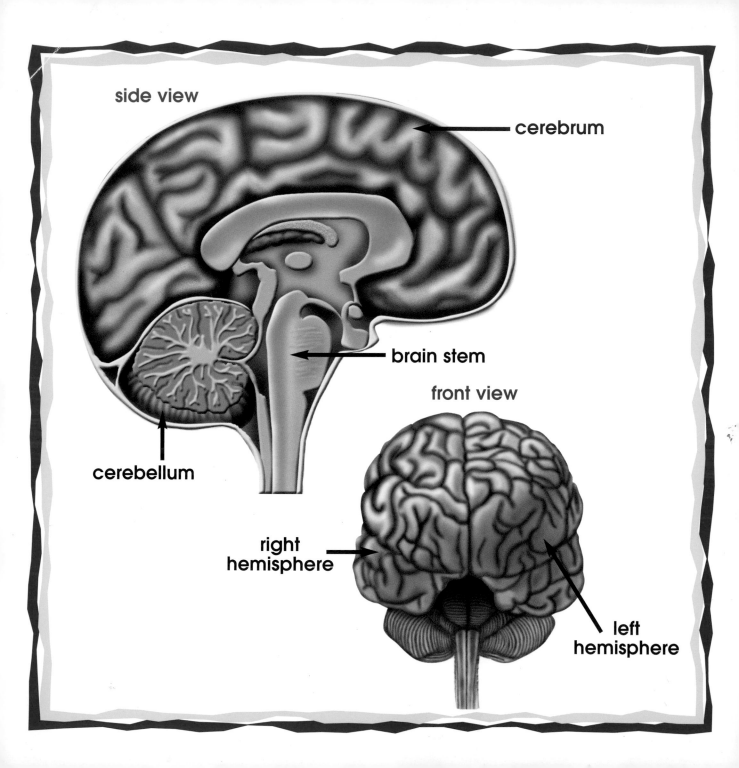

side view

cerebrum

brain stem

front view

cerebellum

right
hemisphere

left
hemisphere

Inside Your Brain

The brain has three main parts. The cerebrum helps you think and feel. It tells your muscles to move. It is divided into two halves called hemispheres. The cerebellum controls balance. The brain stem controls automatic actions such as breathing and blinking.

automatic
happening without you thinking about it

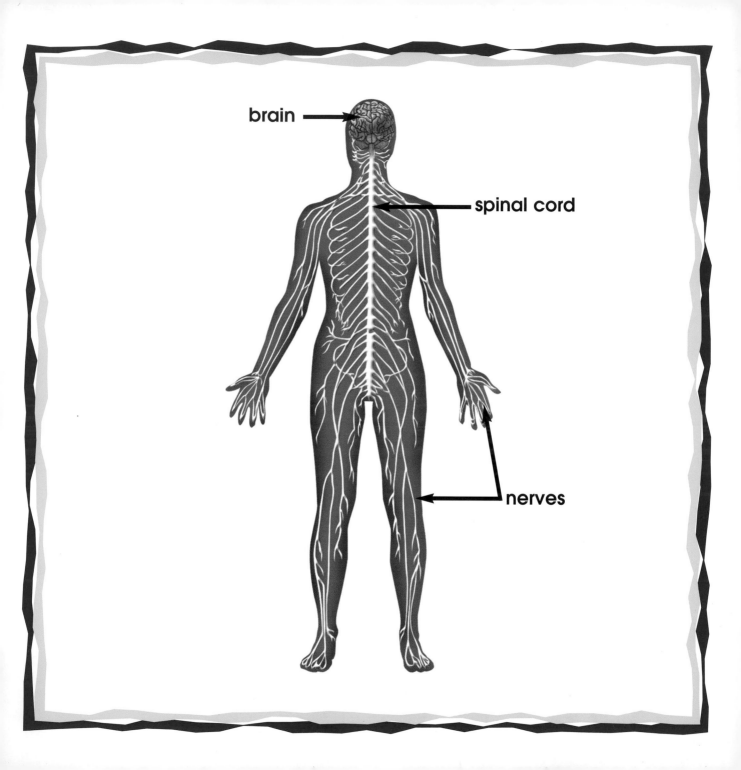

brain

spinal cord

nerves

Your Nervous System

The brain, spinal cord, and nerves make up the nervous system. Your brain sends messages through the spinal cord and nerves. The messages tell your body what to do. Your body sends messages back to the brain.

nerve

one of the thin fibers that sends messages between your brain or spinal cord and the rest of your body

9

Your Brain and Your Senses

Your brain controls your senses. For example, your nerves tell you if water is too hot. The nerves send a message to the brain. The brain tells muscles in your arm and hand to pull back. Messages travel instantly between your brain and other parts of your body.

sense

something that allows you to learn about your surroundings; sight, hearing, touch, taste, and smell are the five senses.

Thinking and Feeling

The cerebrum helps you think and remember. You use your cerebrum to make decisions such as what to wear. Your cerebrum stores your memories. Feelings also come from your cerebrum. Nerve cells in your brain make you feel happy, sad, or scared.

Fun Fact

The right side of your brain controls the left side of your body. The left side of your brain controls the right side of your body.

Your Brain Helps You Move

The cerebellum is the part of the brain that controls movement. It helps you keep your balance while walking. You use your cerebellum while running, riding your bike, and playing sports.

Your Brain Always Is Working

The brain stem controls automatic actions in your body. Your brain stem keeps your body temperature about the same all the time. The brain stem also controls your breathing and heartbeat. Your brain works even when you are asleep.

temperature
the amount of heat or cold in something

Brain Injuries and Illnesses

A neurologist (noo-RAH-luh-jist) is a doctor who treats brain injuries and illnesses. These doctors may help people who fall and hit their heads. Common brain illnesses are seizures, tumors, and infections. A seizure is a sudden loss of body control.

tumor

a lump of tissue in the body that is not normal

A Healthy Brain

You can keep your brain healthy. Stay away from drugs because they can harm your brain. Wear a helmet when you skate or ride your bicycle. Exercise your brain with puzzles or thinking games. Eat healthy food and get plenty of sleep.

Hands On: Test Your Spinal Cord

Your brain sends messages to the rest of your body along the spinal cord. The backbone, or spine, protects the spinal cord. Small bones called vertebra make up your spine. Scientists and doctors label each vertebra with a letter and number. You can test your spinal cord and nerves.

<u>What You Do</u>

1. With one hand, try to touch each finger to your thumb. Next, stick your tongue out and touch your fingers to your thumb. The brain sends messages to do this exercise as far as C5.
2. Bend your elbow. If you can bend your elbow, the message was sent along as far as C7.
3. Tickle yourself around your bellybutton. If you can feel the tickle, the message was sent along as far as T10.
4. Now take off your shoes. Wiggle your toes. If you can wiggle your toes, the message was sent as far as S1.

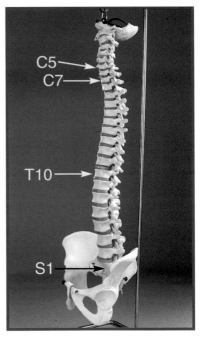

A message for your tongue does not have to travel very far from your brain. A message for your toes has to travel almost to the bottom of your spinal cord. If your spinal cord is hurt, the messages cannot travel below the injury.

Words to Know

brain stem (BRAYN STEM)—the part of the brain located at the bottom of the brain; the brain stem controls automatic body functions.

cerebellum (ser-uh-BEL-luhm)—the part of the brain that controls balance

cerebrum (ser-EE-bruhm)—the main part of the brain where thinking, feeling, and remembering take place

nervous system (NUR-vuhss SISS-tuhm)—the brain, spinal cord, and nerves; the nervous system controls all human body functions.

spinal cord (SPINE-uhl KORD)—a thick cord of nerves that carries signals to the rest of the nerves in the body

Read More

Ballard, Carol. *How Do We Think?* How Your Body Works. Austin, Texas: Raintree Steck-Vaughn, 1998.

Furgang, Kathy. *My Brain.* My Body. New York: PowerKids Press, 2001.

Rowan, Peter. *Big Head!* New York: Alfred A. Knopf, 1998.

Simon, Seymour. *The Brain: Our Nervous System.* New York: Morrow Junior Books, 1997.

Internet Sites

The Brain is the Boss
http://www.kidshealth.org/kid/body/brain_noSW.html
BrainPOP—Brain Movie
http://www.brainpop.com/health/nervous/brain
Neuroscience for Kids
http://faculty.washington.edu/chudler/neurok.html

Index